A Book About My Dog

A Child's Creation

Randi L. Millward

Instructions:

This book is a children's activity book. The sentences are started but left incomplete for the child to finish in his or her own words. The adjacent pages are intentionally left blank for the child to illustrate with his or her own personal artwork.

The artist may color with crayons, tape photos onto the paper, or use any other age-appropriate parent-approved artistic medium that does not bleed through the paper.

ISBN-13: 978-1-943771-08-0
ISBN-10: 1-943771-08-1

More books by this author may be found online at
www.Amazon.com and other participating retailers.

A Book About My Dog

By

_____

Age: _____

Date: _____

My dog is a

_____

_____

_____

_____ .

My dog is named

_____

_____

_____

_____ .

I like when my dog

_____

_____

_____

_____.

My dog likes when I

_____

_____

_____

_____ .

My dog doesn't like

_____

_____

_____

_____.

My dog is really good at

_____

_____

_____

_____.

My dog feels

_____

_____

_____

_____ .

My dog's favorite toy is

_____

_____

_____

_____.

I have fun when my dog and I

_____

_____

_____

_____

My dog barks when

_____

_____

_____

_____ .

My favorite thing to do with my dog is

_____

_____

_____

_____ .

My favorite thing about my dog is

_____

_____

_____

_____.

I wish my dog could

_____

_____

_____

_____

My dog likes to eat

_____

_____

_____

_____ .

When I'm not home, my dog

_____

_____

_____

_____ .

When I come home, my dog

_____

_____

_____

_____

I love my dog because

_____

_____

_____

_____.

The End